Chief Joseph and the Nez Perces

A Photographic History

Bill & Jan Moeller

Mountain Press Publishing Company
Missoula, MT
1995

Second Printing, June 1999

Map by Carla Majernik

Library of Congress Cataloging-in-Publication Data

Moeller, Bill, 1930–
Chief Joseph and the Nez Perces / Bill & Jan Moeller.
p. cm.
Includes bibliographical references and index.
ISBN 0-87842-319-2 (paper : alk. paper)
1. Nez Percé Indians—History. 2. Nez Percé Indians—Government relations. 3. Indians, Treatment of—Oregon—Wallowa County. 4. Joseph, Nez Percé Chief, 1840–1904. I. Moeller, Jan, 1930– II. Title.
E99.N5M56 1995
979.5'730049741—dc20 95-7752
CIP

Printed in Hong Kong by Mantec Production Company

MOUNTAIN PRESS PUBLISHING COMPANY
P. O. Box 2399
Missoula, Montana 59806
406-728-1900

To all our friends and "extended family" in Virginia

❖ Contents

Foreword vii

Preface ix

Acknowledgments xi

Prologue 1

The Flight 13

Epilogue 71

Bibliography 75

Index 77

About the Authors 81

❖ Foreword

The Nez Perce War of 1877 was one of the last great tragedies of the collision between western expansion and the native people who were in its path.

The Nez Perces (a name given them by French fur trappers), or "Nimi-Pu" (also Nee-Me-Poo) as they called themselves, were a powerful, wealthy tribe. Though they peacefully welcomed the white explorers, missionaries, and settlers, their land was soon overrun with them. Treaties forced on the Nez Perces in 1855 and 1862 greatly reduced their homeland. In 1877, after years of abuse, one-third of the Nez Perces were forced to move onto a much smaller reservation. But, just before arriving on the reservation, several young Indians, angry about their mistreatment, reached the breaking point and killed sixteen settlers.

On June 17th the 2nd U.S. Cavalry was sent to punish the Nez Perces. An overexcited volunteer fired on a group of the Indians and the war began.

For nearly four months the Nez Perces fled from the soldiers and volunteers, traveling over 1,500 rugged and spectacular miles through what later became the states of Idaho, Montana, and Wyoming. After fighting twenty battles and skirmishes, usually defeating the soldiers, the Indians were eventually worn down and forced to surrender just forty miles south of Canada and possible sanctuary. General William Tecumseh Sherman called the flight "the most extraordinary of Indian Wars."

Extraordinary it may have been, but the war, in addition to devastating the lives and culture of the Nez Perces, was yet another sad chapter in the record of the growth of the United States.

The Moellers' striking and historically accurate photographs follow the route of the Nez Perces and graphically illustrate what they went through in their pursuit of freedom. The text, mainly in the form of expanded captions, concisely tells the entire story: the events that led to the beginning of hostilities, what happened during the flight, the events that transpired afterwards.

Jock Whitworth

Historian and Superintendent
Big Hole National Battlefield (1988–1993)

—D. F. Barry, University of Montana Mansfield Library Archives

❖ Preface

Of events that happened in the past, written records may be scanty or nonexistent. In the case of Indian-army conflicts, the written records are almost exclusively those of the army and present only one side of the story. Using the research materials available, we have tried to piece together an accurate history of the Nez Perces' epic flight from the army. Depending on the sources, accounts vary slightly on Chief Joseph's surrender. We have used what we consider to be the most widely accepted account.

In reading about the flight of the Nez Perces, you may wonder why they crossed the continental divide so often, each time in a different place. The map will help you better understand the Indians' route; it shows how the divide runs and where the pertinent passes are located.

According to local knowledge, Joseph's birthplace was in the cave we have shown on page 3. The site is not officially recognized as his birthplace, but neither is any other place, and this is the only cave in the area.

Through the photographs, you will be able to appreciate just how arduous was the 1,500-mile journey undertaken by the Nez Perces. We took care to photograph each location as the Nez Perces would have seen it; that is, without any modern elements shown.

Throughout the flight army authorities credited Joseph with being a great military leader. In fact, Joseph had little to do with Nez Perce fighting strategies. Although he was a leader, and he cast a vote as such in the tribal council, he was not a warrior. Joseph was a peacemaker who wanted only what was best for his people, and he always tried to achieve it with diplomacy.

The tale of the Nez Perces, like that of so many Indian tribes, is a sad one. The Nez Perces were friendly to whites and unwarlike, yet they were forced into flight by unjust actions by the army. Their surrender ended the fighting but not their travails. Instead of being returned to their homeland, as the surrender terms stipulated, they were sent to Oklahoma.

Joseph's skill as a diplomat was put to use during his years in exile. The unassuming yet dignified leader crusaded for his people by delivering eloquent speeches. Through his efforts, eventually most of his people—but not Joseph himself—were allowed to return to the Nez Perce reservation in the Northwest.

Chief Joseph, General Oliver O. Howard, and Colonel Nelson A. Miles negotiated the surrender in good faith, but the terms were not honored. For forcing the captured Indians into exile, we lay full blame on the army's high command, Generals William Tecumseh Sherman and Philip H. Sheridan. They ignored the surrender terms as if they had never existed.

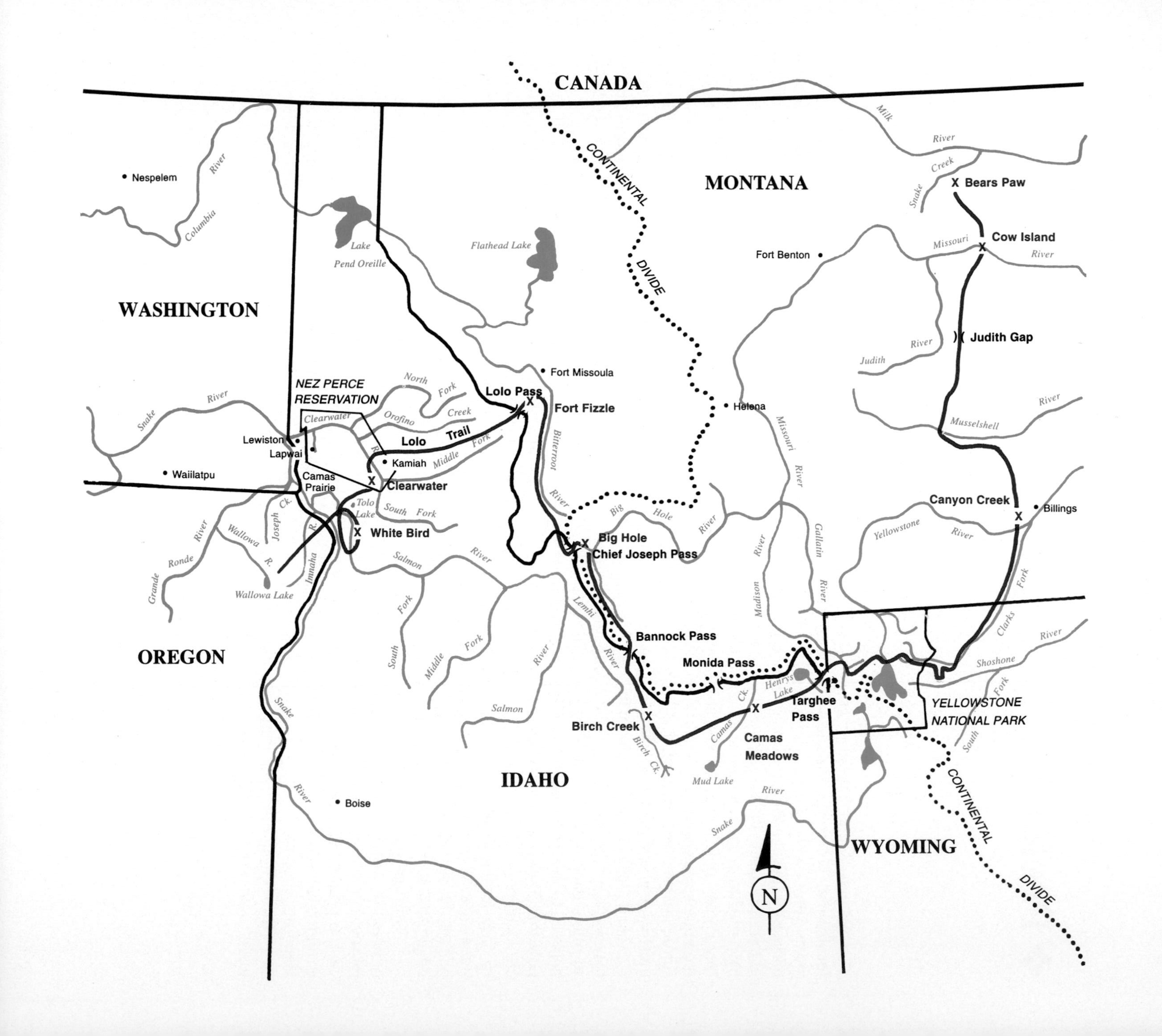
CANADA
MONTANA
WASHINGTON
OREGON
IDAHO
WYOMING
CONTINENTAL DIVIDE
Nespelem
Wailatpu
Lewiston
Lapwai
NEZ PERCE RESERVATION
Camas Prairie
Kamiah
Clearwater
Lolo Trail
Lolo Pass
Fort Missoula
Fort Fizzle
White Bird
Tolo Lake
Big Hole
Chief Joseph Pass
Bannock Pass
Monida Pass
Birch Creek
Camas Meadows
Targhee Pass
YELLOWSTONE NATIONAL PARK
Canyon Creek
Billings
Judith Gap
Cow Island
Bears Paw
Fort Benton
Helena
Boise
Flathead Lake
Lake Pend Oreille
Wallowa Lake
Henrys Lake
Mud Lake
N

❖ Acknowledgments

In compiling the photographs and writing the text for this book, we were fortunate to have the help of many people who willingly shared their knowledge about the Nez Perces with us. We couldn't have done it without their help.

Our thanks to Cheryle Alva, Melinda Ballenger, Marian Buenger, Jodi Deherrera, Charlie Elliott, Tom Geouge, Wayne Jenkins, Gary Kellogg, John Pinegar, Chuck Raddon, and Kathy Thompson of the United States Forest Service; and to Chan Biggs, Buck Damone, Jim Dolan, Sharon Gregory, Bob Lund, David Sisson, and Bert Williams of the Bureau of Land Management. Many of these people provided us with maps and marked the obscure routes we sometimes needed to follow.

Thanks also to Jock Whitworth, Kevin Peters, and Ginny West at Big Hole National Battlefield; to Brian Bull and June W. Greene at Nez Perce National Historical Park; and to Joan Anzelmo and Tom Tankersley at Yellowstone National Park.

Aaron Lytle, whose family owns land on the plateau where the Clearwater Battle took place, kindly allowed us to photograph locations there. And Marge McClaren gave us very good information about the very bad road leading to Hells Canyon, to the point where the Nez Perces crossed the Snake River.

Much of our research has been done in libraries, where we often depended on the valuable assistance of librarians. Our thanks to all of them and especially to Jim Curry of the Parmly Billings Library in Billings, Montana; he was most generous in the time he spent with us.

Our special thanks to Nez Perce Tribal Historian Alan Slickpoo, who filled us in on details about the Clearwater Battle. We appreciate the able assistance of Mountain Press in publishing this book.

Heart of the Monster,
Nez Perce National Historical
Park, East Kamiah, Idaho

Wallowa Lake,
Joseph, Oregon

❖ Prologue

Ages ago, when only animals inhabited the earth, a monster with a voracious appetite dwelt in the Kamiah Valley near the forks of the Clearwater River in what is now the state of Idaho. The monster fed upon the animals, and they lived in fear of being devoured.

One day, Coyote, the leader of the animals, tricked the monster into swallowing him. Once inside the monster's body, he cut out the monster's heart with his stone knife. Coyote carved the monster's body into chunks and cast them over the land. Where they fell, Indian tribes sprang up.

But Coyote missed one place: the monster's homeland. When Fox pointed this out, Coyote sprinkled the beautiful valley with drops of the monster's blood. Thus were created Ne-Mee-Poo, "the People," the Nez Perce tribe.

The Nez Perces

The homeland of the Nez Perces, which they had inhabited for hundreds of years, was located in the valleys watered by the Snake, Clearwater, and Salmon rivers and laced with numerous smaller rivers and streams. The peaks of the Bitterroot Mountains defined the homeland's eastern border and the Wallowa Mountains, west of the Snake River, its southern and western perimeters.

During much of the year the Nez Perces moved from place to place to obtain food, some of which they dried and stored for winter use. Salmon, which ran thick in the rivers during spawning season, and camas root, which grew in the meadows and prairies, were staples of their diet. Sometimes hunting parties crossed the Bitterroots to the open lands beyond, where they found buffalo.

When the Indians were on the move gathering food, they lived in tipis, but they returned to their villages and lived in permanent reed-mat dwellings during the winter.

In the early 1700s the Nez Perces acquired their first horses by trading with tribes to the south. They bred horses for desired traits, raised them on the abundant forage on their lands, and developed large, superior herds. It was not uncommon for one band of Indians to have thousands of horses.

The Coming of the White Men

Although the Nez Perces had previously encountered a few French trappers, their first recorded meeting with white men took place in 1805. An advance

Camas

hunting party from the Lewis and Clark expedition descended the Bitterroots at Weippe Prairie and found Indians gathering camas roots. The rest of the expedition arrived soon after. The Nez Perces took in the tired and hungry men, some of whom were sick, and cared for them until they were able to resume their journey. When the expedition set out again, the Nez Perces supplied them with provisions and dugout canoes, and two guides to show them the way.

In 1811 a group of fur trappers under William McKenzie visited the Nez Perce villages on the Clearwater River. They, too, were well treated by the friendly Indians. McKenzie promised to return and establish a trading post for the Nez Perces. True to his word, McKenzie returned the next year and opened a Pacific Fur Company post. In the years that followed, both American and British/Canadian fur companies, lured by waters rich with beaver, established forts and trading posts near the Nez Perces.

Unlike some Indians, the Nez Perces did not trap beaver themselves. But they traded food and horses with the whites for supplies and goods, including guns. They preferred doing business with the Americans because, unlike the British, they traded freely without regard for fixed prices.

As time passed, the Nez Perces became increasingly dependent on the whites and relied on them for supplies.

Missionaries

The Indians believed that the white man's religion was responsible for his great power. Having seen many whites reading the Bible, the Indians became convinced that the whites' powers emanated from that book; they believed it contained magic.

In 1831 four Nez Perce warriors journeyed with a group of trappers to St. Louis, Missouri, to learn about the white man's religion. Their visit caused much publicity and stirred enthusiasm among the Christian community. Four years later missionaries went west to meet more Nez Perces at the 1835 trappers' rendezvous on Horse Creek, a tributary of the Green River.

Lapwai Creek, Spalding, Idaho

The missionaries found the Indians eager to learn about Christianity. In 1836 a party of Presbyterian missionaries, Dr. Marcus Whitman and his wife, Narcissa, William H. Gray, and Henry and Eliza Spalding, traveled to the Pacific Northwest to establish missions among the Indians. The Whitmans and Gray built their mission at Waiilatpu (near Walla Walla), in Cayuse country. The Spaldings established their mission on Lapwai Creek, in Nez Perce country.

The Nez Perces were so happy for this opportunity to learn the white man's "spirit law" that many of the Indian men, who by custom never performed manual labor, willingly set about felling trees for the construction of the mission house. They dragged logs two miles up from the Clearwater River to the site on Lapwai Creek. Other men of the tribe looked on contemptuously at those who were doing "women's work."

Most of the Nez Perces tried their best to please the Spaldings. Proud to have such an important white man living among them, they attended daily prayer meetings and raptly listened to Bible stories and Spalding's sermons. An interpreter translated for Spalding because he was having trouble learning the Nez Perce language. The Indian congregation learned to sing hymns and accepted their new religion wholeheartedly.

*Mouth of Lapwai Creek,
Spalding, Idaho*

Some of the Indians were disturbed when Spalding, who had no tolerance for Nez Perce culture and tradition, wanted them to give up hunting and take up farming. He preached that unless they changed their ways—such as polygamy, adultery, gambling, and belief in their shamans and spirits—they would be doomed to hell. Spalding sometimes whipped those who disobeyed or would not conform.

Two years after the first mission house was built, Spalding decided he wanted to move. During the construction of his new house on the Clearwater River at the mouth of Lapwai Creek, he had to force the Indians to help with the work.

Despite Spalding's stern and domineering temperament, many of the Nez Perces trusted and admired him. He assisted another missionary in devising a Nez Perce alphabet and dictionary, and they translated parts of the Bible into the Indians' language. By 1839 some of the Indians Spalding taught had converted to Christianity, among them were two chiefs: Tamootsin, named "Timothy" by Spalding, and Tuekakas, whom he called "Joseph."

Joseph frequented the Lapwai mission, even though he had to travel some distance from his home across the Snake River in the Wallowa Valley. He firmly believed in Christianity and carried what he learned back to his people. Spalding visited the valley at Joseph's invitation, and he baptized Joseph's children. One of them, a boy, was born in a cave near the Grand Ronde River early in 1840. When the boy was five years old, he was given the name of his father and became known as "Young Joseph."

The Dissolution of the Missions

Emigrant traffic over the Oregon Trail increased steadily between 1842 and 1847. White settlements sprang up rapidly. The Whitmans encouraged many emigrants to end their journey and establish homes near the Waiilatpu mission and Fort Walla Walla.

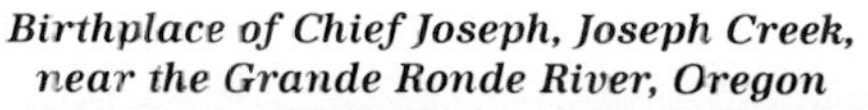

*Birthplace of Chief Joseph, Joseph Creek,
near the Grande Ronde River, Oregon*

Fort Vancouver, Vancouver, Washington

The Cayuses resented the encroachment on their lands and grew increasingly distressed by the intrusive whites. By 1847 their resentment turned to anger after a measles epidemic ravaged their tribe, killing half of them. The disease had arrived with the emigrants. A visiting Indian from the East told the Cayuses that the whites were killing them so they could take their land; the same thing had happened in the East, he said. On hearing this the Cayuses became enraged and attacked the mission, killing the Whitmans and eleven others and taking forty-seven captives, including the Spaldings' daughter, Eliza.

At the time of the attack on Waiilatpu, Spalding was away from his mission at Lapwai. He returned to find it ransacked. Loyal Indian friends took him to his wife, who had taken refuge with other whites in the house of William Craig, a mountain man married to a Nez Perce woman. Craig's father-in-law, Thunder Eyes, kept the whites there for a month in protective custody until a rescue party of Hudson's Bay Company men, led by Peter Skene Ogden, arrived to ransom the Waiilatpu captives.

The Spaldings and other whites in the area then fled west to the safety of Fort Vancouver on the Columbia River.

Peace Council

The massacre brought on the dissolution of the missions, but it did not discourage whites from moving onto Indian lands.

Although the Nez Perces were troubled about white homesteaders, their primary concern in the spring of 1848 was that the American army might be sent against them in retaliation for the massacre at Waiilatpu. Indeed, the Cayuses had asked the Nez Perces and other tribes to help fight a volunteer army marching toward them from the Willamette Valley south of Fort Vancouver. But the American leaders, hoping to avoid an all-out war, called a council with the Nez Perces, the largest tribe in the area.

At the council Old Joseph and other Nez Perce chiefs convinced the Americans of their desire to remain friends with the whites. Joel Palmer, superintendent of Indian Affairs for the Oregon Territory, promised the Nez Perces that no whites would be allowed to live on their lands without their consent. He appointed William Craig as Indian agent for the Nez Perces.

Peace at a Price

After the council the Nez Perces lived in peace with the whites for several years. Many abided by their Christian teachings, while others held onto their traditional customs and beliefs. Joseph's band spent the warm months either camped on the shores of the jewel-like lake at the foot of the snowcapped Wallowa Mountains, or on the banks of the trout- and salmon-filled river that wound through the valley. Before winter they moved to the northeast, out of the valley and into the protection of deep, sheltering canyons.

In 1853, Major Isaac Ingalls Stevens was appointed governor and superintendent of Indian Affairs

Wallowa Lake, Joseph, Oregon

Joseph Creek, north of Enterprise, Oregon

for the newly created Washington Territory. More and more emigrants arrived in the Northwest. In an effort to protect the settlers from potential Indian uprisings, Congress authorized Stevens to define and establish reservations for all the tribes, friendly or not, in the area.

A council was held in May 1855. Stevens presented his plan for the sale of Indian lands and the establishment of reservations. The Indians refused to accept it. They did not want to be displaced in order to provide land for white settlers, and they did not want to be restricted to certain lands. After days of wrangling, however, most of the Indians signed the treaties as drawn up in Stevens's original plan.

The Nez Perces fared better than some of the other tribes. Under the treaty provisions, their reservation boundaries encompassed much of their traditional homeland. Old Joseph's band was given perpetual ownership of the Wallowa Valley.

Indian agency, Spalding, Idaho

Canal Creek, a branch of Orofino Creek, Pierce, Idaho

The Discovery of Gold

In 1860, five years after the signing of the treaties, gold was discovered on a branch of Orofino Creek on the Nez Perce reservation. Prospectors swarmed over the Indian lands, inciting anger among the anti-white faction of Nez Perces while others in the tribe were too busy making money to object to the white invasion and treaty violation. They sold horses and food to the miners and bought whiskey and clothes from them.

A stern-wheeler successfully made its way up the Snake, proving the river navigable for riverboats. Soon the town of Lewiston—nothing more than a tent city at first—was established and named in honor of Meriwether Lewis, William Clark's partner on their famed expedition. By 1862 settlers and miners were firmly entrenched on Nez Perce lands. The whites went so far as to ask the government to remove the Indians so they could have undisturbed access to the area. The Indians, in turn, called for the whites to leave their treaty-protected lands. To keep the peace, the army established Fort Lapwai in the autumn of 1862, near the site of the old Spalding mission.

Courthouse, Pierce, Idaho, 1861

St. Joseph's Mission, Slickpoo, Idaho

The following spring, under pressure from the settlers, Congress called for a council to purchase more land from the Indians. The peaceful Nez Perces took part in the council, but the anti-white factions did not attend. Negotiations dragged on for days because the Indians resisted giving up more of their land. Eventually some of the Nez Perce chiefs signed a new treaty that redefined their reservation, reducing it to one-sixth its former size. The signers became known as the "treaty group." Those who refused to sell their lands and would not sign, including Old Joseph, were called the "nontreaty group."

On the way home from the council, Old Joseph, angry and disillusioned, tore up his copy of the 1855 treaty. He also tore up his most prized possession: a Gospel of Matthew that Spalding had given him when he was baptized and which he always carried with him. To Old Joseph, now, the word of the whites was worthless, and he wanted nothing more to do with their religion.

After the nontreaty group departed, the remaining Nez Perce chiefs signed illegally for the group, thus authorizing the sale of lands they did not own. The 1863 council created much animosity and divided the Nez Perces; however, with the Civil War raging in the East, Congress ignored the treaty, and the Indians continued living several more years as they had, unaffected by government policy. Then, in 1867, after the war ended, Congress ratified the treaty.

For some years following ratification, Old Joseph's band remained in the remote Wallowa Valley, relatively unaffected by white settlers. Old Joseph died in 1871, and on his deathbed he reminded his son and namesake that he had not signed the Treaty of 1863. Since he had not sold his country, he admonished Young Joseph never to sell the land that holds "the bones of your father and mother."

Joseph's Leadership

After Old Joseph's death, the leadership of the Wallowa Valley band of Nez Perces passed to Young Joseph, now thirty-one years old. Like his father, he was known as a peaceful, tolerant man, admired for his logic and wisdom.

In the year Joseph's father died, both Catholic and Protestant missionaries established or reestablished missions on the reservation lands. The various religious sects began bickering with each other, each hoping to claim the glory of the Indians' salvation for themselves.

While many of the reservation Indians remained Christians, many of Joseph's people began to accept the teachings of Smohalla, a shaman prophet who urged them to abandon the ways of the white man. Since the shaman's revelations came from dreams, his followers became known as "the Dreamers."

The white population of the Northwest continued to increase. Gradually, settlers began moving in, especially those who wanted to raise cattle and sheep on the fine grazing lands in the Wallowa Valley. By 1873, many whites had firmly established themselves in the

Presbyterian Church, East Kamiah, Idaho

valley. The prevailing attitude among them was that the government had purchased the land and the Indians should leave.

Joseph met with the settlers several times. He explained that because his father had not signed the treaty, the lands had not been sold. The Indian agent at the time, John B. Monteith, believed that Joseph's band owned the Wallowa Valley and that no whites should be allowed to settle there without the Indians' consent. But he was being pressured by the settlers who wanted the land for themselves.

In the summer of 1873, seeking a compromise, the government divided the Wallowa Valley into two sections—one for whites and one for Indians. But the division satisfied neither side, and did not matter, since the government soon rescinded the order and opened the entire valley to homesteaders. Joseph's people and the other nontreaty bands were told they must move onto the reservation. They refused to go. Many of them favored fighting for their lands, but Joseph hoped to settle matters peacefully.

General hostilities almost erupted after one of Joseph's close friends, Wilhautyah, was murdered. He had been accused, falsely it was later proven, of stealing horses and was killed by two settlers. One of the men who killed him was released and never stood trial; the other was exonerated. Only Joseph's diplomacy kept his warriors from retaliating against the whites. Nevertheless, hot-tempered settlers threatened to scalp Joseph and drive his people from the valley.

In the ensuing years, Joseph steadfastly maintained that the Wallowa Valley had never been sold. After close examination of the 1863 treaty, it was deemed that Joseph was right. But the government still wanted the land and wanted the Indians relegated to the reservation.

In November 1876, a commission was sent to persuade Joseph to sell his lands and move his people to the reservation. He refused to do either. The commission recommended that the Wallowa Valley Nez Perces be given time to move voluntarily, and if they did not comply, force should be used. The government set April 1, 1877, as the deadline.

Joseph was told he must obey the order or troops would be sent against him. He could not believe it, especially since his relations with the military and government officials had been amicable. He tried several times to arrange a meeting with General Oliver O. Howard, commander of the Department of the Columbia. Joseph wanted authoritative confirmation of the order and a chance to explain that so soon after winter it would be impossible for his people to round up their huge herds of horses and cattle in time to meet the deadline. Howard sent word that the deadline would be extended and that he would meet with the nontreaty chiefs on May 3 at Lapwai.

On the appointed date, the Indians met with Howard. The council did not go well. Toohoolhoolzote, an old chief who had been selected as spokesman for the nontreaty chiefs, delivered a long, rambling dissertation that made Howard impatient. The general even had him jailed after they had an argument. Howard felt animosity toward Toohoolhoolzote largely because the old man was a shaman of the Dreamer sect. The power such men held over their followers concerned Howard, a deeply religious Christian. He had no respect for those who were, in his eyes, heathens.

Howard told the Indians the council would change nothing. No matter what they discussed, the Indians would have to move to the reservation; it was the law and he had to enforce it. Howard gave the Indians just thirty days to return to the Wallowa Valley, collect their families and livestock, and move to the reservation.

Joseph, his younger brother, Ollokot, and the rest of the Indians, were stunned and dismayed at Howard's stern dictum. Since he had "shown them the rifle," they would have to give in or fight. Many of the Indians wanted to fight, but the chiefs and elders persuaded them that fighting was useless.

Dispirited to a man, the Indians left the council. Joseph knew he had no choice; to avoid bloodshed he would have to bring his people to the reservation. Uppermost in Joseph's thoughts, however, was how his people would cross the Snake River, now in flood.

Wallowa Mountains, Joseph, Oregon

The Flight

Imnaha River Valley, Imnaha, Oregon

❖ June 1, 1877

It took two full days for Joseph's band to cross the swollen Snake River. After the long trek through the narrow Imnaha River Valley, up steep slopes to the plateau above, then down even steeper slopes to the ford on the Snake, the Indians and their livestock were worn out. Many horses and cattle were swept away during the crossing.

Dug Bar, Snake River, Hells Canyon, Oregon

❖ June 2–12, 1877

With the Snake River now behind them, the Indians still had to cross the rushing Salmon River. After spending a night at a rock shelter used for centuries by their ancestors, the Indians arrived at an ancient campground on the shore of Tolo Lake on Camas Prairie a few miles west of the town of Grangeville. Here they rendezvoused with other nontreaty bands for a few days before continuing on toward the reservation.

One night the Indians held a ceremony, during which some of the young warriors paraded around the campground showing off their war trophies. One of the elders taunted a warrior named Wahlitits for showing off when he had not yet avenged the murder of his father by a white man. Wahlitits brooded all night over what the elder had said. In the morning, Wahlitits and two friends from Chief White Bird's band set out to find the man responsible for his father's death. Unable to find the murderer, they attacked and killed four other white men who were known to hate and mistreat Indians. Around the campfire that night, Wahlitits and his friends boasted of their deed.

Salmon River ford, near Grangeville, Idaho

❖ June 14–16, 1877

News of the killings excited other warriors. Soon seventeen of them, mostly from White Bird's band, formed a war party and set out to avenge other Nez Perces who had been killed or mistreated. Joseph and Ollokot were at the Salmon River butchering some cattle they had left there when they heard about the marauding warriors. Although the brothers set out immediately for the Tolo Lake campground, by the time they arrived only Joseph's band remained; the others had scattered.

Joseph remained overnight, hoping General Howard would arrive. He wanted to explain to Howard that his people were blameless in the uprising and that he still wanted peace. He did not want to fight the whites, but his first loyalty was to the other nontreaty Indians. Howard did not arrive, and Joseph, worried that the general might not believe him if he tried to explain, decided to wait no longer. He hurried his people to break camp and move south to join the other nontreaty bands in the security of White Bird Canyon.

The war parties killed more whites and terrorized others. When General Howard heard what the Indians had done, he assumed only the charismatic Joseph could incite such action among his people. Howard dispatched Companies F and H of the 1st Cavalry, under Captain David Perry, to put down the uprising. As the troops neared White Bird Canyon, a group of volunteers from nearby settlements joined them. Perry was told that unless he moved quickly, the Indians would escape across the Salmon River.

White Bird Canyon,
Nez Perce National Historical Park, Idaho

Tolo Lake, Grangeville, Idaho

White Bird Battlefield, Nez Perce National Historical Park, Idaho

❖ June 17, 1877

In White Bird Canyon, Joseph learned that other Nez Perce leaders agreed with him: they should try to negotiate with the soldiers. Many of the warriors had no guns and, the night before, scouts discovered that the pursuing troops outnumbered them two to one.

In the morning, under a flag of truce, a party of six Nez Perces rode out to meet the troops. The remaining warriors split into two groups and hid behind small, rounded hills to flank the troops as they advanced.

At 4:00 a.m. Perry's command began the steep, four-mile descent into White Bird Canyon. After reaching a low ridge, the advance guard spotted the Indians with the white flag. A volunteer in the group fired at the oncoming Indians, who immediately turned their mounts and galloped for cover. Perry's bugler was among the first casualties; he was killed by one of the hidden warriors. This later hampered Perry greatly in communicating his orders because both of his other buglers had lost their horns.

The volunteers raced down the slope from the ridge, intent on charging the Indian camp near the creek in the valley floor. The warriors forced them back in a panic retreat to a hill on the left of Perry's troops.

As Perry tried to organize and deploy his troops along the east-west-running ridge, Ollokot and a group of Indians sprang from their hiding places and charged H Company on Perry's right flank. The surprised troopers and their horses milled around in confusion. More Indians joined the assault, and within minutes the soldiers and volunteers became separated into small groups, rendering them powerless to stand in force against the onslaught of Indians. By now many soldiers had been killed; the others fled up the canyon in a disorganized retreat with the Indians hot on their heels. Once the soldiers were driven well away from the canyon, the warriors returned to camp.

A third of Perry's command, thirty-four soldiers, had lost their lives. No Indians were killed; three were wounded. The Indians' victory was all the sweeter because they collected a supply of rifles, pistols, and ammunition discarded on the battlefield.

With the Custer massacre of the previous year still fresh in mind, the public was outraged that again Indians had bested trained troops. The press laid all the blame for the army's defeat on Joseph. He was perceived to be the leader of the nontreaty Nez Perces, and this battle made it seem as though they were prepared to wage all-out war.

Joseph had indeed taken part in the battle, but he led no warriors. The Nez Perces, like many other tribes, had no war chiefs to lead unified attacks. Sometimes a war party would select an experienced warrior as leader, but the individuals were under no obligation to follow his orders if they disagreed with them. In battle, generally, each warrior fought as he desired and as his own situation dictated. Joseph was not a war chief; he was not even regarded by his people as a warrior, as was his brother, Ollokot. But Joseph could rightly be called a guardian, since he took charge of directing and shepherding the people when they moved.

Salmon River crossing at Horseshoe Bend, near White Bird, Idaho

❖ June 22, 1877

General Howard had been ordered to capture and punish the Indians who had started the uprising. Since Joseph was presumed to be the leader of all the nontreaty Nez Perces, the military focused on capturing him and the bands he supposedly led.

Howard assembled his force: 227 regulars from units of the 1st Cavalry, the 21st Infantry, and the 4th Artillery; a pack train; two Gatling guns; a mountain howitzer; 20 volunteers; and several treaty Nez Perces to serve as scouts.

After fleeing White Bird Canyon, the Indians crossed the Salmon River nearby at a place called Horseshoe Bend and moved into the high country between the Snake and Salmon rivers. Their number increased with the return of a hunting party from Montana that included two highly respected warriors, Rainbow and Five Wounds.

❖ June 29–July 1, 1877

Howard received a report that Looking Glass, a Nez Perce chief camped with his people along the Middle Fork of the Clearwater River, was recruiting warriors for Joseph and intended to join the warring bands. The report was false, but Howard, unaware of this, sent Captain Stephen Whipple and two companies of cavalry to arrest the chief.

The cavalry charged into Looking Glass's village in the early morning on July 1. Most of the villagers, including Looking Glass, got away unharmed, but the soldiers killed or wounded others and, before they left, looted and destroyed the village. Until now, Looking Glass, like Joseph, had been peaceful and wanted to avoid conflict.

While Whipple and his men attacked Looking Glass's village, Howard and the rest of his command pursued Joseph. They crossed the Salmon River but, encumbered with a pack train and artillery, could not catch up to the Indians.

In councils held after the battle at White Bird Canyon, Joseph favored returning with his people to the Wallowa Valley and, if necessary, fighting there. But the other chiefs wanted to move on and find a place where they could live in peace, and their opinion prevailed. They thought if they moved far away Howard would not bother to follow. They decided to move east, into the Montana Territory.

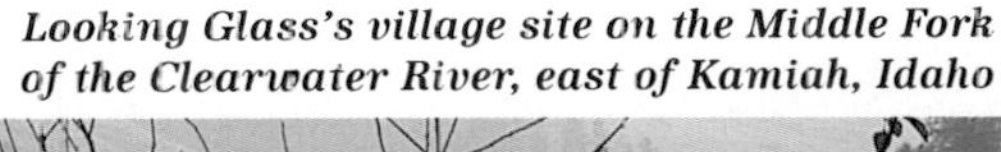

Looking Glass's village site on the Middle Fork of the Clearwater River, east of Kamiah, Idaho

❖ July 4-5, 1877

The Indians headed north and recrossed the Salmon River. They would have to travel east across the broad, open expanse of Camas Prairie before reaching the Bitterroot Mountains and the Montana Territory that lay beyond. Scouts brought word that soldiers—Whipple and his two companies, sent there to protect Howard's supply line—were camped at the small prairie settlement of Cottonwood Station.

The Indians attacked and killed the members of a scouting party sent out by Whipple. The captain made ready to march to the party's relief but thought there were too many Indians to confront with his small force. He pulled back and established a defensive position by having his men dig rifle pits and set up the Gatling guns. By this time Captain Perry arrived with supplies from Fort Lapwai and assumed command.

Warriors circled the army encampment and fired sporadically, keeping the soldiers distracted and confused as they tried to defend themselves. At the same time, under the direction of Joseph and White Bird, Indian women, children, nonfighting men, and livestock streamed across the prairie toward the Clearwater River.

Seventeen volunteers en route to join Perry encountered a war party and were forced into a defensive position. The warriors kept the volunteers pinned down, killing three of them, until the Nez Perce procession had passed by.

Camas Prairie, near Cottonwood, Idaho

❖ July 11–12, 1877

The nontreaty Indians, now dubbed "the hostiles," camped on the west side of the South Fork of the Clearwater River near the mouth of Cottonwood Creek. After Looking Glass and his band joined them, their number swelled to 750 and included 200 warriors.

Howard had broken off his unsuccessful pursuit of the Indians, but when he learned where they were camped, he took his force of more than 500 soldiers and civilian volunteers to the Clearwater. The army crossed the river south of the Indian camp and set up Gatling guns and a howitzer on the bluffs above the camp on the east side of the river.

Howard opened fire, but the height of the bluffs rendered the shots ineffective. The Indians sprang into action and charged across the river to attack the troops as they advanced toward the village. Warriors led by Toohoolhoolzote reached the crest of the bluffs before the soldiers and stopped their advance.

Other warriors, including Ollokot, Rainbow, and Five Wounds, attacked the pack train and nearly succeeded in capturing it. More warriors worked around the army's rear, forcing Howard to regroup his forces on a small plateau. By now the Indians nearly surrounded the soldiers. The soldiers dug in. All day, soldiers and Indians fired back and forth at long distance. Howard's howitzer temporarily drove small groups of Indians from their positions, but they returned when he directed his fire elsewhere. Howard could not break the Indians' siege line.

During the night, many warriors slipped away and returned to their camp to check on their families and livestock. They argued about whether to flee or stay and fight. The majority favored moving the people to a safe place, so in the early morning Joseph led them away.

The warriors held the soldiers in check while gradually withdrawing from the battlefield, which Howard failed to notice. Still thinking he was under siege, the general forged a plan to break out. At 2:30 in the afternoon, as a supply train approached, Howard ordered one unit to charge the Indians' right flank while other troops were to attack the entire Indian line. To Howard's surprise, the line quickly broke. The remaining Indians fled down the bluffs with the soldiers in pursuit. The soldiers reached the village campsite just in time to see the last of the Indians disappearing up a ravine.

Only four Indians were killed in the battle; six were wounded. Howard's casualties totalled fifteen dead and twenty-five wounded. Howard did not pursue the Indians, though it would have been easy to follow their trail. Instead, he allowed his troops to loot and ransack the remains of the village. He did not begin to follow the Indians until the next day.

Bluff above the Clearwater River, Clearwater Battlefield, Stites, Idaho

Clearwater Battlefield, Stites, Idaho

Clearwater River, East Kamiah, Idaho

Weippe Prairie, Weippe, Idaho

❖ July 13–15, 1877

Clear of Howard, the Indians moved north to Kamiah and made ready to cross to the east side of the Clearwater River. The Indians constructed bullboats and ferried the people across the river with the few possessions they had left after their recent quick abandonment of camp. Their 2,000 to 3,000 horses swam across.

The Indians halted at Weippe Prairie at the western foot of the Bitterroot Mountains. While the women gathered camas roots, the chiefs met to deliberate their next move. Joseph still wanted to return to the Wallowa Valley. Looking Glass thought they should cross the Bitterroots on the Lolo Trail and join their friends, the Crows, in their buffalo-hunting lands on the plains. He argued that Howard probably would not come after them when he found out how difficult it would be to move his men, supplies, and guns over the tortuous trail across the mountains. Looking Glass had made many trips to the plains and had never encountered any animosity from the few whites who lived there.

Looking Glass convinced most of the chiefs that his way would prove best. They appointed him as their leader and guide. Joseph, distressed at having to take his people ever farther from their home, reluctantly agreed to Looking Glass's plan.

Hillside above site of Fort Fizzle, Lolo Trail, near Lolo, Montana

Wagon tracks at site of Fort Fizzle, Lolo Trail, near Lolo, Montana

❖ July 23–28, 1877

Word of the Nez Perces' coming preceded them. Howard had telegraphed the commander of Fort Missoula, Captain Charles C. Rawn, and ordered him to build a barricade across the Indians' path and hold them there until he arrived. Rawn's company of forty soldiers and one hundred volunteers constructed a simple log barricade across the trail and waited. The Indians were camped two miles away, in a broad part of the narrow Lolo Creek valley.

Joseph, Looking Glass, and White Bird met with Rawn. The chiefs said the Nez Perces would go peacefully into the Bitterroot Valley if the troops would let them pass. Rawn refused passage unless they surrendered their arms and horses. As soon as Rawn's men heard that the Indians wanted peace, the volunteers deserted the barricade by the dozens.

Since the Indians could not reach an agreement with Rawn, they took matters into their own hands. On July 28, in the dark of night, they climbed the slope to the north of the barricade and simply walked around it. The place where the barricade had been built became known as Fort Fizzle.

Bitterroot River, Lolo, Montana

❖ July 30–August 3, 1877

On July 30, Howard resumed his pursuit of the Indians. He set off with 700 soldiers, his loyal Nez Perce scouts, and a company of axmen from Lewiston to clear the Lolo Trail. By now the Indians were many difficult miles ahead of him and moving south up the Bitterroot Valley.

Before the Nez Perces entered the valley, Looking Glass considered going north to Canada to join Sitting Bull, who had been living there for many months. But that would have meant traveling through Flathead country; although they had been traditional friends of the Nez Perces, some Flatheads had been with Rawn's troops at the barricade and the Nez Perces wondered if they were still allies. They soon found out.

When the Nez Perces reached the Bitterroot Valley, the Flathead chief sent word to Looking Glass to create no trouble or the Flatheads would join the whites against them. The Nez Perces heeded the chief's message. Although many of the settlers in the valley were wary of the Indians, they allowed them to travel its length peacefully and at an easy pace. The Nez Perces found some settlers willing to trade, and they replenished their supplies.

❖ August 8, 1877

Below the Sapphires, stretching for miles, was the wide Big Hole Valley. Nearby mountains rimmed the valley to the north and west; the mountains to the south were just barely visible. The Big Hole River wended through the valley, emptying at its flat, open eastern edge. The valley, at an altitude of nearly seven thousand feet, was uninhabited because of being extremely cold during much of the year.

Looking Glass planned to let the Nez Perces rest here. They could cut and dry lodge poles for their journey to the sparsely treed plains and hunt and fish to replenish their food supply. They arranged their nearly ninety lodges in a flat V-shape on the south side of the North Fork of the Big Hole River where it makes a wide bend to the south, close to the foot of the western mountains. Across the river, to the north, they herded the horses to a treeless hillside that offered excellent pasturage.

Big Hole Valley and Big Hole River, near Wisdom, Montana

Nez Perce village on the North Fork of the Big Hole River, Big Hole National Battlefield, Montana

❖ August 9–10, 1877

Unbeknownst to the Indians, Howard was still on their trail; he entered the Bitterroot Valley as they arrived at Big Hole. But well ahead of Howard was Colonel John Gibbon, who left from Fort Missoula at a fast pace with 197 men.

After crossing the Sapphire Mountains, Gibbon's force had moved forward and was now poised for an attack. Just before daybreak on August 9, his men stealthily strung out along the slope where the horse herd was grazing. The horses moved quietly up the slope, out of the way of the soldiers, and continued to graze. The Indians believed they were safe so had posted no guards. Under whispered orders, the troops crept quietly to the bottom of the slope and into the willow thicket next to the creek. Gibbon ordered them to wait until the first shot was fired; then the entire line was to charge the camp.

Before the troops had fully positioned themselves, a soldier fired a shot at an Indian who was going to check his horses. The troops charged across the North Fork of the Big Hole River into the camp near Joseph's tipi. The attack caught many of the Indians asleep, and, as they groggily rushed from their tipis, the soldiers indiscriminately shot and clubbed any Indian they encountered, including women and children.

The Nez Perce warriors quickly rallied. Many engaged the soldiers in hand-to-hand fighting while others took cover and began sniping at enemy targets.

Lieutenant James H. Bradley, leading the attack on the left flank, was killed in the initial charge. With no one in command, his troops faltered and fell back under heavy fire from the Indians.

On the west side of the camp soldiers tried to burn the tipis, but morning frost covered them and only a few caught fire. Women and children hiding in the tipis killed many of the unsuspecting soldiers.

In the minutes after the attack, many Indians slipped around the flanks of the troops, and some lurked in the brush along the stream. White Bird and Looking Glass, each at opposite ends of the camp, rallied their warriors and pushed the troops toward the center of the camp.

The exposed flanks of Gibbon's command came under heavy attack from paralyzing crossfire. The colonel, now wounded in the leg, was forced to pull his troops back across the river. He moved to a flat, wooded bench at the foot of the mountains to the northwest and ordered his men to dig in. Even there, shielded by trees, Indian sniper fire proved effective and many soldiers were killed. The troops were pinned down. They were almost out of water and now too far from the river to replenish their supply. Neither food nor medical supplies were available because Gibbon, wanting to retain the element of surprise in his attack, had left his noisy pack train back on the trail.

While some troops retreated, others set up a howitzer on the side of the mountain. They fired twice at the village before warriors stormed the gun, killing one soldier, wounding another, and sending the rest fleeing for safety. Then they pushed the howitzer down the mountainside. The gun had come up with the pack train, and on a captured mule the Indians found 2,000 rounds of ammunition.

When the fighting moved away from the camp, Joseph, in his usual role as guardian, gathered the women and children together to make their escape. They collected their horse herd, treated their wounded, hastily buried their dead, and dismantled their tipis before moving out to the south.

The warriors, Ollokot among them, kept the soldiers under siege throughout the rest of the day and all night. At dawn they slipped away to join their fleeing families. They left Gibbon with so many killed and wounded that he was unable to give chase.

Gibbon's force suffered greatly: twenty-nine killed and forty wounded. But the Nez Perce loss was much greater; between sixty and ninety Indians died in the fighting. Of these, only twelve were warriors; the rest were women, children, and elderly.

Looking Glass was blamed for the disaster. He had chosen to take the route that led to Big Hole. He had said that it was safe to rest there. And he, all along, had said that the army would not follow them.

The angry chiefs appointed Poker Joe as their new leader.

Chief Joseph tipi site (horse grazing hill in background), Big Hole National Battlefield, Montana

Howitzer Hill, Big Hole National Battlefield, Montana

Bannock Pass, Centennial Mountains, Leadore, Idaho

❖ August 12–13, 1877

The Nez Perce warriors wanted revenge for their devastating losses at Big Hole. The chiefs counseled restraint, but some of the warriors chose not to heed their advice. A war party attacked a ranch house and killed four of the seven whites there; five miles farther on, two more whites were killed.

The warriors took all the horses they could find, both to replenish their own herd and to prevent any from falling into the army's hands. Now they were sure Howard was on their trail.

The main body of the Nez Perces moved south through the Big Hole Valley, then turned west and again crossed the continental divide in the Beaverhead Mountains at Bannock Pass. They reached the Lemhi River Valley and camped a few miles from a stockaded fort built by white settlers. Looking Glass and White Bird met with the settlers and assured them their people would pass peacefully through the valley if the whites caused them no trouble. The settlers agreed to let them travel through, unimpeded.

Birch Creek Massacre site, northwest of Mud Lake, Idaho

❖ August 15, 1877

An advance guard of Indians moving along Birch Creek to the south, well ahead of the main caravan of Nez Perces, encountered a wagon train. The freighters had stopped for their noon meal. Although the Indians were not initially aggressive, a quarrel developed and turned into a fight, during which the Indians killed all the freighters but one, who escaped. Since the Indians' quarrel was only with the whites, they released two male Chinese passengers. Then the warriors looted and burned the wagons and took the freighters' mules and horses back to the Indian herd.

❖ August 18–20, 1877

Howard arrived at Big Hole Valley the day after the battle. He left his doctors to care for Gibbon and the other survivors and continued his pursuit of the Nez Perces.

Howard suspected the Indians were bound for Yellowstone National Park. In the hope of heading them off, he crossed the continental divide at Monida Pass, many miles southeast of Bannock Pass where the Indians crossed, and sent forty men under Lieutenant George R. Bacon on ahead toward the park along the north side of the continental divide, which runs east-west along the Centennial Mountains. If the Indians eluded Howard, Bacon was to detain them at Henrys Lake, just west of Targhee Pass, which the Indians would have to cross to reach the park.

Howard was not quick enough. After descending onto the upper reaches of the Snake River Plain, his scouts brought word that the Nez Perces were ahead of him, but only by a day's march; they were camped about eighteen miles to the east. The army set up camp between Spring and Camas creeks in Camas Meadows, a broad, grassy area on the predominantly lava-encrusted plain.

The Nez Perce chiefs knew the army was near. The day before, their rear guard had spotted the dust column stirred up by the troops. They sent scouts to find Howard's camp and held a council at which they decided to try to stop the army's pursuit.

In the morning, just before dawn, a large party of nearly two hundred warriors under Looking Glass, Ollokot, and Toohoolhoolzote, departed to run off the army's stock and attack the camp. The party split into three groups: one was to infiltrate the picketed horse herd, free the animals, and run them off; the other two would charge the camp from different directions.

The first group made off with a large part of the herd while the soldiers fired ineffectively in the dark. The Indians soon discovered, to their disgust, that they had captured only part of the herd and that most of the animals taken were pack mules. Upon realizing they had not disabled the cavalry, as they had intended, they were sure Howard would give chase. The warriors established a defensive position along a rough lava ridge about five miles east of the army camp.

Howard ordered the three companies of Captains Camillo C. Carr, James Jackson, and Randolph Norwood to saddle up and give chase under the command of Major George Sanford. About a thousand yards from the Indians' line, the soldiers dismounted and began firing. While Sanford concentrated on the Indians in front of him, other warriors flanked him on the right and left. As soon as he realized what was happening, he ordered a retreat. The three companies were spread out over such a wide area that Norwood's company became separated from the other two.

Norwood intended to retreat but found his way cut off by the Indians. He was forced to take cover in a nearby hollow, in a low outcropping of lava where a few aspen trees provided scanty cover; some of his men took advantage of natural indentations in the lava for rifle pits. The Indians pinned down the soldiers for several hours with long-range rifle fire. By the time Howard arrived with reinforcements, the warriors, unable to dislodge Norwood's men, had withdrawn. No Indians, and only one soldier, were killed in the Camas Meadows engagement.

Again, Howard was thwarted. He could not follow the Indians until he replaced the pack mules the Indians had stolen. And again, he credited the effective attack to Joseph's leadership.

Norwood's Hollow,
Camas Meadows,
Kilgore, Idaho

Rifle pit, Norwood's Hollow,
Camas Meadows, Kilgore, Idaho

❖ August 22, 1877

Joseph led the Nez Perces across the sagebrush flats and over Targhee Pass, where they crossed the continental divide for the third time.

Bacon had arrived at Henrys Lake ahead of the Indians, but after waiting there for two days without seeing any sign of them, he started back to rejoin Howard.

Henrys Lake, Idaho

Targhee Pass, Idaho/Montana

Firehole Falls, Yellowstone National Park, Wyoming

❖ August 22–23, 1877

The Nez Perces entered Yellowstone National Park on a seldom-used hunting trail. They became confused as to their location, so they set up camp and sent out two scouts, Yellow Wolf and Otskai, to find the trail. While scouting along the Madison River, they heard the sound of someone chopping wood. They crept through the trees and captured the wood chopper, John Shively, a prospector on the way to the Montana goldfields, and took him back to their camp.

Yellow Wolf and several other scouts set out again, following the Firehole River and looking for more whites. When darkness fell, they made camp and soon found they were not far from other campers, whose fire they could see through the trees. Since being established in 1872, the park had attracted many tourists.

❖ August 24, 1877

In the morning Yellow Wolf and his scouts rushed the camp and easily overwhelmed the nine white tourists there. Among those taken prisoner were Frank Carpenter; his two sisters, Mrs. Emma Cowen and thirteen-year-old Ida Carpenter; his brother-in-law, George F. Cowen; and J. Albert Oldham. They were taken back to the Nez Perces, who were on the move again, traveling east toward the Yellowstone Valley. After the chiefs held a council, Poker Joe told the captives they could go free if they agreed not to spy for the army; the Indians did not want their location reported.

The tourists set off after they had been stripped of their guns and saddles and their good mounts exchanged for worn-out Nez Perce horses. When two of the horses played out, their riders took the opportunity to disappear into the woods. The Indian scouts who had been trailing the freed captives rode up to the tourists and demanded to know where the two had gone. An argument developed, and the Indians shot and wounded Cowen and Oldham. During the commotion, two more of the whites and the slightly wounded Oldham escaped into the woods. Poker Joe arrived on the scene in time to prevent what could have become a massacre of the remaining whites.

Poker Joe told Carpenter and his sisters they would have to come with him back to the Indian camp. Cowen was left for dead. When the tourists arrived at the camp, they were given over to Joseph's care. They were terribly distressed over the fate of Cowen, but Joseph's kind and friendly manner impressed them nevertheless.

Firehole River, Yellowstone National Park, Wyoming

❖ August 25, 1877

The Indians followed Trout Creek to the Yellowstone River and continued south along the Yellowstone to Buffalo Ford. That evening they crossed to the eastern bank of the river.

Trout Creek, Yellowstone National Park, Wyoming

Buffalo Ford, Yellowstone River, Yellowstone National Park, Wyoming

❖ August 26, 1877

In the morning, after the chiefs had once again met to decide the tourists' fate, Poker Joe gave the captives old, slow mounts and set them free. They eventually encountered an army detail that escorted them to Bozeman. The hardy Cowen survived and was reunited with his wife a month later. The Indians detained the prospector, John Shively, for a week before allowing him to leave.

Poker Joe, having traveled through the area several times before, was leading the Indians through the park on a long, rough wilderness route, well away from settlers and army posts.

As the main body of Nez Perces traveled northeastward, toward the forbidding Absaroka Range, small bands of warriors ranged through other sections of the park. Acting on their own, and without the chiefs' knowledge, they attacked a party of tourists near the Mud Volcano. One tourist was killed; the others escaped north to Mammoth Hot Springs, only to be attacked by another party of Nez Perce warriors. Another tourist was killed, then the warriors headed far to the north and burned the buildings on a ranch. On their way back to join the main group of Nez Perces, they partially burned the Baronett Bridge that spanned the Yellowstone River.

Clarks Fork Canyon from Dead Indian Hill, west of Clark, Wyoming

❖ September 8–10, 1877

Howard made good time along a well-worn Indian trail while the Nez Perces struggled through steep, rocky terrain littered with deadfalls and made their way down precipitous cliffs.

Nez Perce scouts kept the chiefs abreast of the army's movements. They knew the position of Howard's scouts in their rear and that Sturgis's troops were ahead of them at the entrance to Clarks Fork Canyon.

The Indians traveled southeast along the rim of the canyon above the Clarks Fork and crossed the eastern end of Sunlight Basin. Their route would take them to Sturgis's position, less than ten miles to the east, and they knew they could not slip past him in that open country without being seen.

The chiefs formulated a plan to take advantage of the terrain. To reach the plain east of Clarks Fork Canyon, they would have to cross Dead Indian Hill to the south. Branching off the hill's southern slope was a trail that led south to the Stinking Water River. When the Nez Perces reached this fork, they went a short distance along the trail toward the Stinking Water, then milled their animals around to conceal their trail and confuse anyone who tried to track them. They then doubled back to the north, leaving the trail and taking to the timber, and entered a gulch on the east side of Dead Indian Hill that led them back to the Clarks Fork.

The rocky gulch was so narrow that in places two horses could barely walk abreast. The Indians and livestock picked their way through its dark depths, dropping a thousand feet in a quarter mile. The gulch's northern egress, a veritable slit between steep walls, was formed eons ago by a waterfall that eventually wore away the precipice over which it plunged.

Sturgis had become impatient with waiting. He took his entire force and headed for the Stinking Water, twenty-six miles to the south, to look for the Indians. He had gone ten miles when his scouts, who had surveyed the countryside from a high mountain, returned and reported that they had seen the Nez Perces on the trail to the Stinking Water. Sturgis hastened on to the river.

When he reached the Stinking Water he saw no evidence of the Nez Perces. Either his scouts had been mistaken or he had been tricked. He started his troops back along the way they had come. Soon, his advance scouts brought word that Howard was ahead of him at the entrance to Clarks Fork Canyon.

When Howard arrived at the point where the Indians milled their horses, he stopped to examine the tracks. He deduced that the Indians had doubled back on their trail. He followed them through the gulch, but by this time the Nez Perces were far ahead of him.

Floor of Clarks Fork Canyon, west of Clark, Wyoming

Mouth of Clarks Fork Canyon, west of Clark, Wyoming

❖ September 11–12, 1877

The Nez Perces left the rough country of Clarks Fork Canyon and continued following the river through the valley. In two days they were fifty miles to the north, at the confluence of the Clarks Fork and the Yellowstone River.

Looking Glass had gone ahead to hold councils with the Crows. After counting on their friendship, he was dismayed to learn that the Crow chiefs sided with the whites. The Nez Perces had no choice now but to head for Canada, traveling all the way through country inhabited by Indians who were no longer their friends.

The embarrassed Sturgis, after a forced march, joined Howard, who assumed command of the joint forces. Believing Sturgis would exert special effort to redeem himself after the Stinking Water fiasco, Howard sent him after the Nez Perces. He also sent a dispatch to Colonel Nelson A. Miles at Fort Keogh on the Yellowstone, more than two hundred miles to the northeast, ordering him to depart immediately so he could place himself between the Indians and Canada.

❖ September 13, 1877

On their way north through more settled country, Nez Perce war parties raided white settlements, stole horses, and killed whites to keep them from reporting the Indians' whereabouts to the army.

The rest of the Indians crossed the Yellowstone River and headed toward Canyon Creek, which flows through the Yellowstone Valley before spilling into the Yellowstone River to the south. A few miles to the northwest, the creek exits a narrow canyon. The Indians intended to move up the canyon to reach the hilly plain above the valley. The creek valley is partially encircled by rimrock cliffs and broken by shallow ravines, gullies, and washes.

Here Sturgis finally caught up with the Nez Perces. He sighted them from a ridge two miles away. His advance guard reached the rear of the Indian train about four miles below the mouth of the canyon. The warriors immediately formed a defensive line across the rear to prevent the cavalry from charging the women, children, and horse herd. To the warriors' surprise, the troops dismounted and began fighting on foot, thus forfeiting momentum and any advantage they might have had. The warriors held the soldiers in check with long-range fire from horseback, all the while moving slowly backward to shield the retreating people. Other warriors on the rimrock aided them by pouring a murderous fire onto the troops below.

Sturgis tried a flanking maneuver by ordering a battalion to charge and cut off part of the horse herd and the retreating warriors before they reached the mouth of the canyon. Twice the soldiers charged, and twice the Indians drove them back. Unhindered, the people and the horses disappeared into the canyon.

When all the Indians had reached safety in the main canyon and started moving toward the top of the bluffs through a narrow side canyon, the rear guard erected barricades of brush, rocks, and logs across the trail.

Since it was nearly dark, Sturgis stopped at the mouth of the canyon and made camp.

Canyon Creek, Laurel, Montana

❖ September 14–17, 1877

In the morning Sturgis resumed his pursuit of the Indians, but the barricades in the canyon slowed him down. A body of Crow and Bannock scouts had moved out well ahead of the main force, however, and they dogged the heels of the Nez Perces, harassing them, stealing horses, and engaging the warriors in running battles.

After thirty-seven miles Sturgis, weary from marching hard for a week trying to catch the Nez Perces, found that the Indians were well ahead of him. By the time he reached the Musselshell River and found that the Indians had increased their lead considerably, he gave up the chase. His tired troops and worn-out horses could go no further.

Musselshell River, Ryegate, Montana

Big Snowy Mountains, Judith Gap, Montana

❖ September 19, 1877

Now less than two hundred miles from the Canadian border, the Nez Perces pressed doggedly on. The going was easy for many miles before and after they passed through broad Judith Gap that separates the Big Snowy Mountains on the east and the Little Belt Mountains on the west.

Nez Perce war parties continued raiding ranches for horses. They also captured several hundred head from a small band of Crows camped to dry buffalo meat from a recent hunt.

❖ September 23, 1877

Covering seventy-five miles in thirty-six hours, the Nez Perces made the gradual climb to the high, broken country above the Missouri River. From there they descended the wind-sculpted bluffs to the crossing at Cow Island.

A small detachment of soldiers was stationed on the island to guard a supply depot. Cow Island Landing was head of navigation on the Missouri during the low-water season—in the fall—and much freight had accumulated.

As a party of twenty Nez Perce warriors crossed, the soldiers nervously watched from their hastily constructed fortifications. They made no attempt to interfere, so the other Indians and the horse herd forded the river. When all had crossed, the Indians moved two miles up Cow Creek and camped.

Two Indians went to the soldiers to ask if they could buy some food. The sergeant offered them a side of bacon and a half bag of hardtack, but that meager amount could not possibly feed all the hungry Indians. Provoked by his niggardly offer, warriors waited until dark and then began shooting at the guards. The soldiers returned fire and shooting continued throughout the night. Meanwhile, the Indians looted the piles of freight and got away with much-needed food and supplies. What they didn't take, they burned.

Earlier the chiefs had told the warriors not to fire unless the soldiers fired first. The warriors had ignored the chiefs then, and ignored them again when the chiefs protested against the looting. The warriors' attitude was that as long as they were at war with the whites, it was fair to take their supplies.

Cow Island, Missouri River, Montana

❖ September 24, 1877

In the morning the Indians moved on. After ten miles they encountered and captured a wagon train. Three teamsters were killed; the others with the train escaped.

When word reached Fort Benton, farther west on the Missouri River, that the Indians were headed for Cow Island, Major Guido Ilges and a detachment of thirty-six volunteers had set out to intercept them. After Ilges reached Cow Island Landing and saw what the Indians had done to the depot, he hurried after them and quickly caught up to them.

A rear guard of warriors attacked the small detachment, and, after a brief skirmish in which one volunteer was killed, Ilges ordered a quick retreat; his men were no match for the Indian sharpshooters.

That night in the Nez Perce camp, Looking Glass argued with Poker Joe. He complained that Poker Joe was setting too fast a pace; the people were tired and needed a rest. Poker Joe reluctantly relinquished leadership to Looking Glass but warned him that if they rested, the army would probably catch them and kill them all.

❖ September 25–29, 1877

The weather deteriorated. A frigid wind blew from the north. Looking Glass allowed the tired people to slow their pace; the hunting was good in this country and he thought Howard was far behind.

After passing through the low, treeless Bear Paw Mountains, the Indians camped a few miles farther north, on the east side of Snake Creek. This tributary of the Milk River runs through a shallow depression with low bluffs cut by gullies rising to the east and south. Treeless except for small willows growing along the creek, the only available fuel was bison chips. Looking Glass made the decision to camp here, but many of the Indians did not like the place. It was just forty miles from Canada.

Bear Paw Battlefield, Nez Perce National Historical Park, south of Chinook, Montana

❖ September 30, 1877

Colonel Miles had been on the march from Fort Keogh since September 18. In the early hours of this cold Sunday morning, his Cheyenne scouts discovered the Nez Perce camp. Two hours later Miles's cavalry units attacked in a pincer movement.

Warriors had rushed to the bluff tops when they realized troops were advancing. They hid behind rocks and ridges and waited for the charging soldiers. Three companies of the 7th Cavalry on detachment with Miles charged the camp from the south. At two hundred yards the Indians opened fire and stopped the charge cold. The soldiers fell back, regrouped, and began another charge, this time farther to the east in a flanking movement along a ridge above the Indian camp. After intense fighting, including hand-to-hand combat, the troops had sustained heavy losses and were again repelled by the Indians. Miles ordered a third charge. This time troops swept over the edge of the bluffs and into part of the Indian camp, where Joseph and others, fighting at close range, determinedly drove them back up the bluff.

The other prong of the pincer movement was more successful. Sioux and Cheyenne scouts accompanied by three companies of the 2nd Cavalry charged into the horse herd while Nez Perces frantically tried to gather their animals. The horses scattered, and most of them fell into the hands of the cavalrymen.

The Indians stubbornly resisted throughout the day. Eventually forced to pull back his troops, Miles established a siege line around the Nez Perce camp. By the end of the day, the Indians had lost twenty-two men, women, and children—among them Ollokot, Toohoolhoolzote, and Poker Joe. Of the main chiefs, only Joseph, White Bird, and Looking Glass remained. Miles reported twenty-three killed and forty-five wounded—20 percent of his total force.

While Miles's troops dug in, so did the Indians. They dug deep pits along the creek to protect the women and children. It was snowing and bitterly cold, but the Indians built no warming fires lest the flames provide targets for army snipers.

When Miles first attacked, some of the Indians had been packed and ready to go. They escaped, and others slipped away during the night. Indians who stayed suffered, cold and hungry, as they waited through the long night.

Bear Paw Battlefield, Nez Perce National Historical Park, south of Chinook, Montana; ridge where Indians and army fought

Bear Paw Battlefield, Nez Perce National Historical Park, south of Chinook, Montana; Indian camp, looking southwest to Surrender Hill

❖ October 1, 1877

By morning five inches of snow covered the ground. A strong, frigid wind whistled in from the north. Although some desultory long-range firing occurred during the morning, it did little damage to either side.

At noon, after the snow and wind had slackened somewhat, Miles displayed a flag of truce. He wanted to talk with Joseph.

Joseph and several armed warriors met with Miles in his tent. They discussed terms of a surrender, but talks broke down when Miles demanded too many concessions, including that the Indians relinquish all their weapons. The warriors departed, but Miles asked Joseph to stay for more discussion. In violation of the flag of truce, Miles took Joseph prisoner. He was tied, hand and foot, then taken from the tent and left outside with the mules.

Under orders from Miles, Lieutenant Lovell Jerome was reconnoitering the Nez Perce camp at about the time the Indians were becoming suspicious because Joseph had not returned. When the Indians learned that Joseph was being held prisoner, they detained Jerome. Unlike the treatment accorded Joseph, however, they treated Jerome courteously.

Bear Paw Battlefield, Nez Perce National Historical Park, south of Chinook, Montana; Joseph's camp on Snake Creek; Indian rifle pits located on ridge in background

Bear Paw Battlefield, Nez Perce National Historical Park, south of Chinook, Montana; Indian rifle pit

❖ October 2, 1877

In the morning Miles decided to exchange prisoners. After the exchange, hostilities resumed. The Indians suffered greatly from the cold and the lack of food. Water, too, was difficult to obtain, so many did without. The soldiers were relatively comfortable; they had enough food and their tents were warm.

❖ October 3, 1877

The siege continued. The chiefs discussed their options. Looking Glass had sent riders to find Sitting Bull, who was camped in Canada near the border, just north of the Nez Perces, to enlist his aid.

Hoping the Sioux would come to their rescue, Looking Glass and some others did not want to surrender; other chiefs, however, thought it would be best for the women and children if they did so. Even after the rough treatment Joseph received from Miles, he wanted the Indians to lay down their arms and surrender in accordance with Miles's terms.

White Bird opposed a surrender; he was sure all the chiefs would be hung as leaders of the uprising. Nothing had been resolved by the time Looking Glass went out to have a smoke in a rifle pit. He saw an Indian riding in from a distance. Thinking it might be a Sioux messenger, he stood up for a better look and was shot dead by a sniper.

Since White Bird was too old, Joseph assumed the role of leading chief. Only now was he finally in the position Howard had ascribed to him all along.

Bear Paw Battlefield, Nez Perce National Historical Park, south of Chinook, Montana; Looking Glass's rifle pit, and rock where Oolokot was killed

❖ October 4, 1877

In the evening, Howard arrived at Miles's camp with a small detachment in advance of his main force.

He received a chilly reception from Miles, who figured that Howard, as the senior officer, would get all the credit and the glory if the Nez Perces surrendered now. But Howard assured Miles he would not take command; Miles could continue to direct the operation. Miles relaxed and they discussed their strategy.

Howard's main force would arrive the next day. If the Nez Perces still refused to surrender, the army would then have enough men to storm the camp and prevail.

❖ October 5, 1877

Howard sent two Nez Perce scouts under a flag of truce to carry a message to Joseph: If the Indians surrendered, they would be taken to Fort Keogh for the winter and in the spring they would be allowed to return to their homeland. Miles had said much the same thing when he met with Joseph four days earlier.

Joseph sent the scouts away while he, White Bird, and several subchiefs deliberated. White Bird still firmly believed the whites could not be trusted, but Joseph prevailed; he summoned a scout and sent word to Howard that he would surrender.

In the afternoon, Joseph mounted his horse and led five warriors on foot to the place where Miles and Howard waited. Clad in ragged garments, he dismounted slowly, with much dignity, extended his arm, and presented his rifle as a token of the surrender.

Bear Paw Battlefield, Nez Perce National Historical Park, south of Chinook, Montana; Surrender Hill

With an interpreter translating, Joseph said:

Tell General Howard I know his heart. What he told me before I have in my heart. I am tired of fighting. Our chiefs are killed. Looking Glass is dead. Toohoolhoolzote is dead. The old men are all killed. It is the young men who say yes or no. He who led the young men is dead. It is cold and we have no blankets. The little children are freezing to death. My people, some of them, have run away to the hills, and have no blankets, no food; no one knows where they are—perhaps freezing to death. I want time to look for my children and see how many of them I can find. Maybe I shall find them among the dead. Hear me, my chiefs. I am tired; my heart is sick and sad. From where the sun now stands, I will fight no more forever.

Bear Paw Battlefield, Nez Perce National Historical Park, south of Chinook, Montana; plaque at surrender site

Afterward, the other Nez Perces filed into the army camp and surrendered their weapons. In the warmth of the campfires that had been built for them, the Indians ate their first hot meal in six days.

During the night, White Bird and most of his people slipped away and headed for Canada.

❖ Epilogue

The pursuit and capture of the Nez Perces cost the government nearly a million dollars and the lives of 111 whites. The Indian losses were even greater. In addition to the 96 Nez Perces that had been killed, 36 of them women and children, they had lost virtually everything they owned: their lands, their homes, their horses, and most of their possessions.

During several interrogations Joseph explained how his people had made repeated efforts to avoid hostilities. Miles was impressed with the leader's eloquence, directness, honesty, dignity, and kindness.

Two days after Joseph's surrender the Indians began the long overland journey to Fort Keogh. They would remain there for the winter, since it was deemed too costly to move them back to the reservation during the cold, snowy months.

On October 15 the caravan reached the fort. Miles saw to it that the Indians had a desirable camping site and he treated them well. Both Miles and Howard assumed the Nez Perces would be returned to the Northwest as soon as weather permitted.

Within days of their arrival at Fort Keogh, however, General Philip Sheridan ordered the Nez Perces sent downriver by flatboat to Fort Abraham Lincoln on the Missouri River in Dakota Territory. Sherman concurred with the order. He thought the Indians should never be allowed to return to Lapwai and that their leaders should be executed, believing such harsh treatment would set an example and quell rebelliousness in other tribes.

After a race to reach their destination before the river froze, the Indians arrived at Fort Lincoln on November 16. A week later they were loaded onto a train and taken to Fort Leavenworth, Kansas, where they were interned as prisoners of war.

During the Nez Perce flight from the army, the supposed and actual exploits of Joseph had been reported in newspapers throughout the country and he had become a noted figure. On the way to Fort Leavenworth, many people—literally thousands in St. Paul—thronged the railroad stations to get a look at the famous Chief Joseph. Joseph complained that his arm ached from shaking so many hands.

At Fort Leavenworth the Indians were forced to camp in a swampy area beside the Missouri River. One observer compared the place to the infamous Andersonville Civil War prison. The cold, damp site—a breeding ground for disease—sorely affected Joseph's people, many of whom were already sick when they arrived. In December Joseph petitioned the government. He stated the plight of his people and requested permission to return to the Nez Perce reservation in Idaho Territory. Sherman ignored the petition.

In the spring, after 21 of the remaining 431 Nez Perces had died, Congress got around to debating their fate. On May 27, 1878, a bill was passed providing for the removal of the Nez Perces to Indian Territory. By July they had been transported by train and wagon to the Quapaw Reservation in the northeast corner of what later became Oklahoma. The Nez Perces spent a year on the reservation. They had no shelter, no medicine to fight the malaria they had contracted, and found that no crops would grow in the infertile ground. Within months, 47 more of Joseph's people had died and many more were ill.

While on the reservation, the Nez Perces were joined by 80 more of their tribe—some of whom had escaped to Canada at the time of Joseph's surrender but, homesick, had been rounded up on their way back to Lapwai.

In July 1879 the remaining 370 Nez Perces were moved 180 miles west, to a wooded, fertile site on the Salt Fork of the Arkansas and Chickaskia rivers in the land of the Poncas.

Joseph and another Nez Perce chief, Yellow Bull, were allowed to travel to Washington and plead their case for being returned to their homeland. They met with the secretary of the Interior, Carl Schurz, who was sympathetic to their cause, and with many members of Congress. But the western senators did not want the Indians living in their areas and blocked any action that would have put the Nez Perces back in their homeland.

Although Joseph's trip to Washington achieved no changes in government policy, it effectively revealed the sad condition of the Nez Perces to the public. As a result of pressure from Indian sympathizers and the Presbyterian church, in 1883 twenty-nine Nez Perces, mostly widows and orphans, were given permission to return to their homeland. Congress made no provision for their travel expenses, so the Indians raised the money themselves by selling handicrafts. A wave of sympathy swelled for the Indians, and Congress received fourteen petitions from various humanitarian groups demanding that the Nez Perces be returned to their homeland. The Senate duly amended the Indian Appropriations Bill to allow for the Nez Perces' return.

On May 25, 1885, the Nez Perces boarded a train bound for the Northwest. The 118 who agreed to become Christians could go to the Lapwai agency. The others were sent to Nespelem, on the Colville Indian Reservation in Washington Territory.

Many settlers in Oregon and around the vicinity of Lapwai still held Joseph and his Wallowa Valley band solely responsible for the killings that occurred when the Nez Perce troubles began, eight years earlier. That animosity prevented Joseph and his people from being allowed to return to Lapwai; they were sent to the Colville reservation for their own safety. At Colville, where they settled on Nespelem Creek, the Nez Perces had no shelter and did not receive their fair share of food, clothing, and supplies. But they overcame these hardships, persevered, and eventually became successful farmers and cattle breeders.

Joseph never gave up the hope of returning to the Wallowa Valley. He pleaded his case to whomever he thought could help him. He gave speeches and granted interviews to journalists who sought him out. In 1897 he took his case to President William McKinley and the Indian Commission in Washington, D.C. In 1900 the Indian inspector, James McLaughlin, was sent to investigate the situation, and he took Joseph with him to the Wallowa Valley. Joseph hoped to purchase land for his people to live on, but McLaughlin thought it unwise because of the lingering hostility settlers in the area felt toward the Wallowa Nez Perces.

Joseph returned to Colville and never saw his homeland again. On September 21, 1904, at age 64, the broken-hearted leader died. Even in death, his most cherished wish was denied: he is not buried in the Wallowa Valley where his father lies, but at faraway Nespelem.

Chief Joseph's grave, Nespelem, Washington

❖ Bibliography

Brady, Cyrus Townsend. *Northwestern Fights and Fighters*. Reprint. Garden City, New York: Doubleday, Page & Company, 1913.

Beal, Merrill D. *"I Will Fight No More Forever," Chief Joseph and the Nez Perce War*. Reprint. New York: Ballantine Books, 1989.

Brown, Mark H. *The Flight of the Nez Perce*. Reprint. Lincoln: University of Nebraska, 1982.

——. *The Plainsmen of the Yellowstone: A History of the Yellowstone Basin*. Reprint. Lincoln: University of Nebraska Press, 1969.

Chalmers, Harvey, II. *The Last Stand of the Nez Perce: Destruction of a People*. New York: Twayne Publishers, 1962.

Feathers, Joseph J. S., ed. *These Are the Nez Perce Nation*. Lewiston, Idaho: Lewis-Clark Normal Press, 1970.

Fisher, S. G. "Journal of S. G. Fisher," in *Contributions to the Historical Society of Montana*, Vol. 2. Helena: State Publishing Company, 1896.

Garcia, Andrew. *Tough Trip Through Paradise, 1878-1879*. Edited by Bennett H. Stein. Sausalito, California: Comstock Editions, 1986.

Haines, Aubrey L. *Historic Sites Along the Oregon Trail*. Gerald, Missouri: The Patrice Press, 1981.

Highlights of the Upper Missouri National Wild and Scenic River, Lewis and Clark National Historic Trail. Bureau of Land Management. Lewiston, Montana.

Howard, Helen Addison. *Saga of Chief Joseph*. Reprint. Lincoln: University of Nebraska Press, 1978.

——. *War Chief Joseph*. Reprint. Lincoln: University of Nebraska Press, 1964.

Howard, O. O. *Nez Perce Joseph*. Reprint. New York: Da Capo Press, 1972.

Josephy, Alvin M., Jr. *Nez Perce National Historic Trail*. Washington, D. C.: Government Printing Office, 1990.

——. *The Nez Perce Indians and the Opening of the Northwest.* Reprint. Lincoln: University of Nebraska Press, 1979.

Kelly, Luther S. *Yellowstone Kelly.* Edited by M. M. Quaife. Reprint. Lincoln: University of Nebraska Press, 1973.

McLaughlin, James. *My Friend the Indian.* New York: Houghton, Mifflin Company, 1910.

McWhorter, L. V. *Hear Me My Chiefs! Nez Perce History and Legend.* Reprint. Caldwell, Idaho: The Caxton Printers, 1986.

——. *Yellow Wolf: His Own Story.* Reprint. Caldwell, Idaho: The Caxton Printers, 1986.

Nez Perce Country. United States Department of the Interior. Washington, D.C.: Division of Publications, National Park Service, 1983.

❖ Index

Absaroka Range, 47, 48
Andersonville Civil War prison, 71
Arkansas River (Salt Fork), 72

Bannock Indians, 56
Bannock Pass, 38, 40
Bear Paw Battle, 62–69
Bear Paw Mountains, 60
Beaverhead Mountains, 38
Bacon, George R., 40, 42
Baronett Bridge, 47, 48
Big Hole Battle, 36–38
Big Hole River, 34; North Fork, 34, 36
Big Hole Valley, 34, 38
Big Snowy Mountains, 57
Birch Creek, 39
Bitterroot Mountains, 1, 22, 27, 28, 29
Bitterroot Valley, 30, 31, 32, 40
Bozeman, Montana Territory, 47
Bradley, James H., 36
Buffalo Ford, 46

Camas, 1, 2
Camas Creek, 40
Camas Meadows, 40
Camas Prairie, 15, 22
Canada, 31, 52, 57, 60, 66, 69, 72
Canyon Creek, 54
Carpenter, Frank, 45
Carpenter, Ida, 45
Carr, Camillo C., 40
Cayuse Indians, 2, 4
Centennial Mountains, 40
Chickaskia River, 72

Civil War, 8
Clark, William, 7
Clarks Fork (of the Yellowstone River), 48, 50–51, 52
Clarks Fork Canyon, 48, 50–51, 52
Clearwater Battle, 24
Clearwater River, 2, 3, 22; Middle Fork, 21; South Fork, 24
Colville Indian Reservation, Washington Territory, 72
Congress of the United States, 6, 8, 71, 72
Cottonwood Creek, 24
Cottonwood Station, 22
Councils: (1855), 6; (1863), 8; peace council (1848), 4
Cowen, Emma, 45, 47
Cowen, George F., 45, 47
Cow Island, 58, 60
Craig, William, 4
creation myth (Nez Perce), 1
Crow Indians, 27, 52, 56, 57
Custer massacre, 19

Dakota Territory, 71
Dead Indian Hill, 50–51
Dreamer sect, 8, 10

Firehole River, 44
Five Wounds, 20, 24
Flathead Indians, 31
Fort Abraham Lincoln, 71
Fort Benton, 60
Fort Fizzle, 30
Fort Keogh, 52, 62, 68, 71

Fort Lapwai, 7, 9, 22, 72
Fort Leavenworth, 71
Fort Missoula, 30, 36
Fort Vancouver, 4
Fort Walla Walla, 3
fur companies, 2

Gibbon, John, 36, 40
Grande Ronde River, 3
Grangeville, Idaho Territory, 15
Gray, William H., 2

Henrys Lake, 40, 42, 48
Horse Creek, 2
Horseshoe Bend, 20. *See also* Salmon River
Howard, Oliver O., 9, 10, 16, 20, 21, 24, 27, 28, 33, 36, 40, 42, 48, 50, 52, 66, 68, 69
Hudson's Bay Company, 4

Ilges, Guido, 60
Imnaha River Valley, 14
Indian Appropriations Bill, 72
Indian Territory (Oklahoma), 71

Jackson, James, 40
Jerome, Lovell, 64
Joseph, Old (Tuekakas), 3, 4, 6, 8
Joseph, Young, 3, 8, 9, 10, 14, 16, 19, 20, 21, 22, 27, 30, 36, 40, 42, 45, 62, 64, 66, 68, 69, 71, 72
Judith Gap, 57

Kamiah, Idaho Territory, 27

Lamar River Valley, 48
Lapwai (Fort) Nez Perce Indian Agency, 72
Lapwai Creek, 2, 3
Lapwai mission, 2, 7
Lemhi River Valley, 38
Lewis, Meriwether, 7
Lewis and Clark expedition, 2
Lewiston, Idaho Territory, 7, 31
Little Belt Mountains, 57
Little Wind River, 48
Lolo Creek Valley, 30
Lolo Pass, 29
Lolo Trail, 27, 28, 31
Looking Glass, 21, 24, 27, 30, 31, 33, 34, 36, 38, 40, 52, 60, 62, 66, 69

Madison River, 44
Mammoth Hot Springs, 47
McKenzie, William, 2
McKinley, William, 72
McLaughlin, James, 72
Medicine Tree, 32
Merritt, Wesley, 48
Miles, Nelson A., 52, 62, 64, 66, 68, 71
Milk River, 60
missionaries, 2–4, 8
Missouri River, 58, 60, 71
Monida Pass, 40
Montana Territory, 21, 22
Monteith, John B., 9
Mud Volcano, 47
Musselshell River, 56

Nee-Me-Poo (the People), 1
Nespelem, Washington Territory, 72
Nez Perce Indians 1, 2, 3, 4, 6, 7, 8, 15, 16, 19, 31, 34, 36, 38, 39, 47, 50–51, 54, 58, 69, 71, 72
Nez Perce Reservation, Idaho Territory, 71
nontreaty group, 8, 15, 16, 19, 24, 28, 68
Norwood, Randolph, 40

Ogden, Peter Skene, 4
Oldham, J. Albert, 45
Ollokot (Joseph's brother), 10, 16, 19, 24, 36, 40, 62
Oregon Trail, 3
Orofino Creek, 7
Otskai, 44

Pacific Fur Company trading post, 2
Palmer, Joel, 4
Perry, David, 16, 19, 22
Poker Joe, 32, 36, 45, 47, 60, 62
Ponca Indians, 72
Presbyterian church, 72

Quapaw Reservation, Indian Territory, 71

Rainbow, 20, 24
Rawn, Charles C., 30, 31

St. Louis, Missouri, 2
St. Paul, Minnesota, 71
Salmon River, 15, 16, 20, 22
Sanford, George, 40
Sapphire Mountains, 33, 34, 36
Schurz, Carl, 72
scouts: Cheyenne, 62; Howard's Nez Perce, 28, 31, 50; Sioux, 62
Sheridan, Philip, 71
Sherman, William Tecumseh, 48, 71
Shively, John, 44, 47
Shoshone (Stinking Water) River (North Fork), 48, 50–51
Sioux messenger, 66
Sitting Bull, 31, 66
Smohalla, 8
Snake Creek, 60
Snake River, 1, 7, 10, 14, 20, 40
Spalding, Henry, 2, 3, 4, 8
Spalding, Eliza, 2, 4
Spalding, Eliza (daughter), 4
Spring Creek, 40
Stevens, Isaac Ingalls, 4
Stinking Water (Shoshone) River, 48, 50–51
Sturgis, Samuel D., 48, 50, 52, 54, 56
Sunlight Basin, 50

Targhee Pass, 40, 42
Thunder Eyes (Craig's father-in-law), 4
Timothy (Tamootsin), 3
Tolo Lake, 15
Toohoolhoolzote, 10, 24, 40, 62, 69
treaty group, 8
Treaty of 1855, 8
Trout Creek, 46

United States Army Units:
  1st Cavalry, 16, 20; Troops F and H, 16, 19
  2nd Cavalry, 62
  4th Artillery, 20
  7th Cavalry, 48, 62
  21st Infantry, 20

Wahlitits, 15
Waiilatpu mission (Walla Walla), 2, 3, 4
Wallowa Lake, 4
Wallowa Mountains, 1, 4, 6
Wallowa Valley, 8, 9, 10, 27, 72
Washington, D.C., 72
Washington Territory, 6
Weippe Prairie, 2, 27
Whipple, Stephen, 21, 22
White Bird, 15, 16, 22, 30, 36, 38, 62, 66, 68, 69
White Bird Battle, 19–20
White Bird Canyon, 16, 19, 20, 21
Whitman, Marcus, 2, 3, 4
Whitman, Narcissa, 2, 3, 4
Wilhautyah, 9
Willamette Valley, 4

Yellow Bull, 72
Yellowstone National Park, 40, 44
Yellowstone River, 46, 47, 52, 54; Clarks Fork of, 48, 50–51, 52
Yellowstone Valley, 54
Yellow Wolf, 44, 45

❖ About the Authors

Bill and Jan Moeller are professional photographers, researchers, and writers. Since 1982 they have traveled full time in their RV to visit and photograph battlefields and other historical sites, and to write books about the two primary influences currently affecting their lives: western history and recreational vehicles.

Before embarking on this land-based venture, they lived aboard a sailboat for twelve years and circumnavigated the eastern United States—up the Hudson River to the Great Lakes, down the Mississippi to the Gulf of Mexico, and back to the eastern seaboard. During that time they wrote two books: *Living Aboard: The Cruising Sailboat as a Home* and *The Intracoastal Waterway: A Cockpit Cruising Handbook*. Their more recently published RV books are: *A Complete Guide to Life on the Open Road*; *RV Electrical Systems*; and *RVing Basics*. In addition, they write a weekly syndicated newspaper column called "RV Traveling."

Chief Joseph and the Nez Perces is the fourth photographic history book the Moellers have written. Earlier books using the same unique approach include: *The Oregon Trail: A Photographic Journey*; *Crazy Horse, His Life, His Lands: A Photographic Biography*; and *Custer, His Life, His Adventures: A Photographic Biography*.